```
I0067385
```

If you find yourself coming to North Texas on the third Wednesday of any month, go to https://www.SuccessNorthDallas.com/speakers/ and consider joining us as our guest.

Being a Catalyst for Success

The Fulfilling Life of a Servant Leader

Bill Wallace

**Foreword by
Tom Leppert**

THiNKaha®

An Actionable Servant Leader Journal

E-mail: info@thinkaha.com
20660 Stevens Creek Blvd., Suite 210
Cupertino, CA 95014

Copyright © 2018, Bill Wallace

All rights reserved. No part of this book shall be reproduced, stored in a retrieval system, or transmitted by any means other than through the AHAthat platform or with the same attribution shown in AHAthat without written permission from the publisher.

⇨ Please go to
http://aha.pub/SuccessCatalyst
to read this AHAbook and to share the individual AHAmessages that resonate with you.

Published by THiNKaha®
20660 Stevens Creek Blvd., Suite 210, Cupertino, CA 95014
http://thinkaha.com
E-mail: info@thinkaha.com

Photography by Misty

First Printing: December 2018
Hardcover ISBN: 978-1-61699-299-6   1-61699-299-9
Paperback ISBN: 978-1-61699-298-9   1-61699-298-0
eBook ISBN: 978-1-61699-297-2   1-61699-297-2
Place of Publication: Silicon Valley, California, USA
Paperback Library of Congress Number: 2018962420

Trademarks

All terms mentioned in this book that are known to be trademarks or service marks have been appropriately capitalized. Neither THiNKaha, nor any of its imprints, can attest to the accuracy of this information. Use of a term in this book should not be regarded as affecting the validity of any trademark or service mark.

Warning and Disclaimer

Every effort has been made to make this book as complete and as accurate as possible. The information provided is on an "as is" basis. The author(s), publisher, and their agents assume no responsibility for errors or omissions. Nor do they assume liability or responsibility to any person or entity with respect to any loss or damages arising from the use of information contained herein.

Acknowledgement

To my best friend Jan Klodner, without whom Success North Dallas would not have flourished nor become the organization that is today positioned to move forward for many more years to come.

To all my Success North Dallas friends and family who have accompanied me on this extraordinary thirty-year journey, embracing all of the ups and downs, celebrating the ninety companies and nonprofits founded, the 1,000 jobs created or found, the 100-plus books authored, and the 360 incredible domestic and international speakers who have stepped up to our lectern month after month.

To all those who are carrying the DNA of Success North Dallas and Servant Leadership to future generations.

Most importantly, thank you to the God I serve.

Dedication

I'd like to dedicate this book to these people I hold dear:

- Jennifer Mallon, who came alongside of me and made this book a reality.

- Dr. William Branton Wallace, my son, for teaching me.
- Matthew Alexander Wallace, my son, for inspiring me.
- William Rhodes Wallace, my grandson, for whom this book is really written.

How to Read a THiNKaha® Book

A Note from the Publisher

The AHAthat/THiNKaha series is the CliffsNotes of the 21st century. These books are contextual in nature. Although the actual words won't change, their meaning will every time you read one as your context will change. Be ready, you will experience your own AHA moments as you read the AHA messages™ in this book. They are designed to be stand-alone actionable messages that will help you think about a project you're working on, an event, a sales deal, a personal issue, etc. differently. As you read this book, please think about the following:

1. It should only take 15–20 minutes to read this book the first time out. When you're reading, write in the underlined area one to three action items that resonate with you.
2. Mark your calendar to re-read this book again in 30 days.
3. Repeat step #1 and mark one to three more AHA messages that resonate. They will most likely be different than the first time. BTW: this is also a great time to reflect on the AHAmessages that resonated with you during your last reading.

After reading a THiNKaha book, marking your AHA messages, re-reading it, and marking more AHA messages, you'll begin to see how these books contextually apply to you. AHAthat/THiNKaha books advocate for continuous, lifelong learning. They will help you transform your AHAs into actionable items with tangible results until you no longer have to say AHA to these moments—they'll become part of your daily practice as you continue to grow and learn.

Mitchell Levy, The AHA Guy at AHAthat
publisher@thinkaha.com

THiNKaha®

Contents

Foreword

Unfortunately, there are far too few "servant leaders." Communities need them, and they truly make a difference outside of the bright lights and cameras. Bill Wallace is a good example of one who leads by serving.

I have had the pleasure of both knowing and working with Bill Wallace for a number of years. He has always sought to make our community better, in some ways that are very visible but often behind the scenes. He was one of the founding fundraisers and supporters of the Ronald McDonald House in Dallas and a founding father of Bryan's House. Both of these organizations serve Dallas citizens who have unique and pressing medical needs. Currently, he is involved with the organization, "Night of Superstars," which touches the most vulnerable in our community by giving them any opportunity to see a brighter tomorrow.

Bill also understands the values of relationships and how important they are to leverage in bettering a community. Through Success North Dallas, he has acted as a mentor for many and used that organization to model community service for others. Success North Dallas fosters the notion of "paying it forward" and "giving back." These principles come from Bill and his philosophy of giving, which I have witnessed for many years.

Success North Dallas provides a venue for business people, non-profit professionals, and students to come together and build solid and mutually beneficial relationships. For all the years I have known Bill, he enables mentoring relationships among people that span a broad range of disciplines. The atmosphere of helping others, which you will find at any Success North Dallas event, is a reflection of Bill and his commitment to the Dallas community and giving to others.

Tom Leppert

Money is nice, but living a good life is not defined by money. A good life is determined by how you feel when you go to sleep at night and when you wake up in the morning.

Bill Wallace
http://aha.pub/SuccessCatalyst

Share the AHA messages from this book socially by going to http://aha.pub/SuccessCatalyst.

Section I

Netweaving:
Living and Working a Good Life

Each one of us wants to live a good life. In our quest to do so, we often find ourselves asking questions like, "How can I live a good life?" or "What does it mean to live a good life?" It may sound complicated, but it's really not.

Some people think that living a good life is determined by how much money you make or how many properties you own. There's no denying that having money is nice, but that doesn't define what a good life is. It is not just about money, but how you feel each waking moment. Put simply, "Are you fulfilled?"

A good life can also be determined by the smiles that appear on the faces of others every time they see you. You live a good life if you put others ahead of yourself, and you have their best interests at heart.

Watch this video: http://aha.pub/SuccessCatalystS1.

1

If we're only present for ourselves, we're going nowhere; however, being there for others further defines our presence for ourselves.

_____

_____

_____

2

Money is nice, but a good life is not defined by money. It is determined by how you feel when you go to sleep at night and when you wake up in the morning.

_____

_____

_____

3

Living a good life is determined by the smiles that appear on the faces of others every time they see you, and they keep that smile after you've gone.

_____

_____

_____

4

When two people meet each other, that's networking. When two people start intertwining their networks, that's #Netweaving. Are you doing it?

_____

_____

_____

5

When networking, start a conversation by giving the person the opportunity to talk about themselves and think of who you can connect this person to. #Netweaving

_____

_____

_____

6

#Netweaving is all about building relationships by helping others with their needs in mind rather than just your own. Are you helping others?

_____

_____

_____

7

#Netweaving energizes you and makes you better at everything you do, because you're doing it for other people.

_____

_____

_____

8

#Netweaving is based on the belief that what goes around comes around. When you help other people, help will come to you when you need it. Are you helping others?

_____

_____

_____

9

Is there someone you know who would benefit from knowing or meeting the person in front of you? #Netweaving

_____

_____

_____

10

Does the person you're interacting with right now have valuable information that they can provide to someone else you know? #Netweaving

_____

_____

_____

11

With #Netweaving, you build and enrich your career by helping others build theirs.

_____

_____

_____

A great leader is not necessarily the one who does the greatest things but the one who gets other people to do the greatest things.

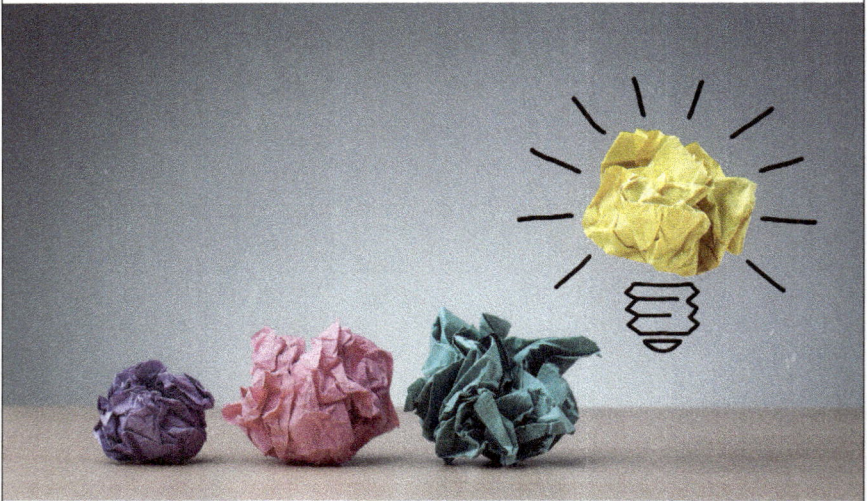

Bill Wallace
http://aha.pub/SuccessCatalyst

Share the AHA messages from this book socially by going to http://aha.pub/SuccessCatalyst.

Section II

Servant Leadership:
A Life You Can Be Proud Of

If you're in a leadership position, do you ask yourself, "How can I be a better leader?" Good leaders are those who inspire other people to do great things. Before you can become a good leader, you first need to become a good servant.

A servant leader is one who serves other people first. To be a servant leader, you have to have this natural feeling of putting other people first and helping them. A servant leader actually receives more because it's the heart that's receiving.

Watch this video: http://aha.pub/SuccessCatalystS2.

12

The happiest people in life are the givers, not the getters. #BeAGiver

_____

_____

_____

13

You can have everything you want in life if you just help other people get what they want. #BeAGiver

_____

_____

_____

14

The more we put other people first, the more we become first. The more we help, the more we are helped.

_____

_____

_____

15

When we seek to discover the best in others,
we also bring out the best in ourselves.

_____

_____

_____

16

A great leader is not necessarily the one
who does the greatest things. A great leader
is the one who gets other people to do the
greatest things.

_____

_____

_____

17

A great leader's actions inspire others to dream more, learn more, do more, and become more. Are you inspiring other people?

_____

_____

_____

18

The best way to lead people is to walk behind them. #LeadFromBehind

_____

_____

_____

19

A good leader must first become a good #ServantLeader. Are you serving others?

_____

_____

_____

20

A #ServantLeader is a servant first, beginning with the natural desire to help other people.

_____

_____

_____

21

#ServantLeadership is when you start leading by helping others. Are you helping others?

_____

_____

_____

22

#ServantLeadership is when you put the
interests of others at the
center of your decisions.

_____

_____

_____

23

#ServantLeadership is not about "I" or "we."
It's about "them."

_____

_____

_____

24

A #ServantLeader empowers others first so that they may empower themselves. Empower other people!

_____

_____

_____

25

You know that you're a real #ServantLeader when you see the people you've served come through the door of that early-morning meeting 30 minutes early and stay 30 minutes afterward because you have served them. #Inspire

_____

_____

_____

26

#Leadership is about making others better as a result of your presence and ensuring that the impact lasts in your absence.

_____

_____

_____

27

You know you're a #ServantLeader if you
lead with the heart of a servant.

_____

_____

_____

28

When you live life as a #ServantLeader,
those around you will naturally rise with
your servant's tide. #ServeToSucceed

_____

_____

_____

29

A life you can be proud of is when you lead with, "How can I help?" How often do you help others?

_____

_____

_____

30

You know you live a life you can be proud of when you come to work as a servant, not as a king or a CEO. Do you work as a servant or as a king?

_____

_____

_____

31

A significant life is about serving those who benefit from your gifts, your leadership, and your purpose. #SharingIsCaring

_____

_____

_____

32

A life you can be proud of is when there are more people smiling when you leave than when you arrived.

_____

_____

_____

33

A life you can be proud of is when you leave a place better than you found it. #LeavingALegacy

_____

_____

_____

34

A life you can be proud of is when there are more people loving and helping each other when you leave than when you arrived. #LeavingALegacy

_____

_____

_____

35

You become a better person if you're a servant leader. If you have a group of people who all have servant attitudes, you impart a breadth of good to the world. #BeBetter

_____

_____

_____

36

A servant life is truly a life you can be proud of, because it's a life that is the most loved, the most genuine, the most powerful, and the most successful.

_____

_____

_____

37

When you lead with a servant's heart, you
receive a lot more, because
it's your heart that's receiving.

_____

_____

_____

38

A great leader doesn't give greatness to
others. A great leader helps bring out the
greatness that is already inside of them.

_____

_____

_____

Share the AHA messages from this book socially by going to
http://aha.pub/SuccessCatalyst.

Section III

Running a Business You Can Be Proud Of

Running a business takes a lot of hard work, but running a business you can be proud of not only requires hard work but also passion. When you love what you do, you will find yourself having fun. You wake up each morning excited to start working.

A business you can be proud of makes you excited, not only because you get to share your work, goals, and vision with others but also because your goal is not just to make money, but to make a difference.

Watch this video: http://aha.pub/SuccessCatalystS3.

39

Great things in business are never done by just one person. They're done by a team.

_____

_____

_____

40

You don't build a business; you help build
people up, and then
the people build the business.

_____

_____

_____

41

A business you can be proud of is created when the people in your team are working well together. Does your team work together?

_____

_____

_____

42

A business you can be proud of is one where
your team loves helping other people first.
Are people on your team servant leaders?

_____

_____

_____

43

The #Culture of your company is defined by the worst possible behavior the CEO will tolerate from any one employee. What's your company's culture?

_____

_____

_____

44

Your company's #Culture is determined by your internal business practices—what you will and will not tolerate.

_____

_____

_____

45

Protect the culture of your company even if
you sometimes need to make sacrifices.

_____

_____

_____

46

When your company's culture dies, there
are always two deaths. First, the culture, and
second, the company. #ProtectYourCulture

_____

_____

_____

47

Culture triumphs over everything, even the best balance sheet. What's your company's culture?

_____

_____

_____

48

A business you can be proud of is one that puts a smile on your face when you are creating something for yourself and for others. Are you smiling?

_____

_____

_____

49

A business you can be proud of is one that creates opportunities for others that guide them to succeed.

_____

_____

_____

50

A business you can be proud of is one that elevates highly successful people to move to the next level, while allowing equal opportunity for all.

_____

_____

_____

51

You have a business you can be proud of
when you're excited to share the ownership
of your vision with other people
to make them a part of it.

_____

_____

_____

52

Do you want a business you can be proud of? Take away the things you're focusing on that you don't love, and start doing what you really love to do.

_____

_____

_____

53

You have a business you can be proud of when you wake up each morning excited to go to work. Are you excited about work when you wake up?

_____

_____

_____

54

You have a business you can be proud of when you're excited to share your vision and your passion with the world.

_____

_____

_____

55

You have a business you can be proud of when you're excited to meet with your friends and talk about your business and the people you work with.

_____

_____

_____

56

You have a business you can be proud of when you're excited to share what you do for other people. Are you excited to share your work?

_____

_____

_____

57

A business you can be proud of is one where your goal is not just to make money but to make a difference.

_____

_____

_____

58

Great business owners don't set out to be leaders but to make a difference. It's not about the role; it's about the goal.

_____

_____

_____

59

A long life means nothing if you don't spend it helping other people and making a difference. Are you making a difference?

_____

_____

_____

60

The first step in making a difference is believing that you have the ability to change the world one genuine interaction at a time. #BelieveYouCan

_____

_____

_____

61

If you're crazy enough to think you can change the world, you can and you will.

_____

_____

_____

62

Inspire others, and let them know that they can make a difference. Are you inspiring others?

_____

_____

_____

63

You don't have to be brilliant or rich to make a difference in someone else's life. You just have to #Care.

_____

_____

_____

Share the AHA messages from this book socially by going to
http://aha.pub/SuccessCatalyst.

Section IV

Giving Back to the Community

The quote, "What goes around, comes around," has been said for centuries. The saying simply means that when you give, you also receive, which is why giving is an endless cycle.

In this day and age, giving back to the community is a necessity. It's also often what millennials look for in a company. When we give back without expecting anything in return, we become better versions of ourselves and our companies.

Watch this video: http://aha.pub/SuccessCatalystS4.

64

If you give to the community without expectation, the gifts that may come back from that are countless. Are you giving back with no expectation of return?

_____

_____

_____

65

Those who give without any expectation are the givers who truly receive. #GiveBack

_____

_____

_____

66

Giving back to the community is about being vulnerable and being transparent; it's about taking risks. Are you taking risks?

_____

_____

_____

67

Community leadership has many definitions. What is yours?

_____

_____

_____

68

Culture trumps all. The culture of your company is defined by the worst possible behavior that you, the CEO, will tolerate from any one employee or team.

69

What do you want to improve in your community? Think about it and take action. That's how you can #GiveBack.

_____

_____

_____

70

Setting yourself apart from the herd can be as simple as volunteering for a non-profit organization. #GiveBack

_____

_____

_____

71

You can give young people the chance
to set themselves apart from the herd by
showing them how to attain their goals.
Then take a step back and
let them do it. #GiveBack

_____

_____

_____

72

You can show young people that they can
be different, and let them
know that it's okay. #GiveBack

_____

_____

_____

73

What do millennials look for in a company? They look for companies that are giving back to the community.

_____

_____

_____

74

If #GivingBack to the community is not part of your corporate culture, you may not survive in this day and age.

_____

_____

_____

75

A company that only focuses on money may fail, but a company that focuses on giving back to the community will succeed. #GiveBack

_____

_____

_____

76

#GivingBack is an investment in your community, your people, and yourself. Are you investing?

_____

_____

_____

77

When you're #GivingBack something that you're passionate about, you're really just giving to yourself. Giving goes full circle.

_____

_____

_____

78

We make a living with what we get, but we make a life with what we give. #GiveBack

_____

_____

_____

79

#GivingBack to the community is not just about making a donation; it's about making a difference.

_____

_____

_____

80

It is only through giving for the right reasons that we are able to receive more. Are you giving?

_____

_____

_____

81

When you give back to the community, you make a huge difference in other people's lives and a continued difference in your own.

_____

_____

_____

82

You can measure a person's life by how much effect they have on others. How are you affecting others?

_____

_____

_____

83

We rise by lifting others up. #LiftPeopleUp

_____

_____

_____

84

Success is finding satisfaction in giving a
little more than you take.

_____

_____

_____

Our mistakes don't define who we are; how we acknowledge and correct them does.
#OwnYourMistakes

Bill Wallace
http://aha.pub/SuccessCatalyst

Share the AHA messages from this book socially by going to
http://aha.pub/SuccessCatalyst.

Section V

Handling Things When It Hits the Fan

In life, things happen—both good and bad. When good things happen, typically, our reactions are that we become happy and we celebrate. But life is not always good. Bad things can happen too.

As human beings, we make mistakes every now and then. Those mistakes don't define who we are; our reactions do. What do you do when things get messy? Do you deny your mistakes and fight the situation, or do you acknowledge your mistakes and fix them?

Watch this video: http://aha.pub/SuccessCatalystS5.

85

Our mistakes don't define who we are. How we acknowledge and correct them does. #OwnYourMistakes

_____

_____

_____

86

Stuff happens to all of us all the time.
It's just part of life.

_____

_____

_____

87

Resistance is persistence. The longer you fight the situation, the more energy you will spend on fighting it. This will leave you with less energy to change it.

_____

_____

_____

88

You can learn a lot from your mistakes when you aren't busy denying them. #OwnYourMistakes

_____

_____

_____

89

Acknowledging that you messed up is the first step in overcoming the situation (persisting in it), because you can't fight it and fix it at the same time. #OwnYourMistakes

_____

_____

_____

90

Own your mistakes. When you do, you will respect yourself more and so will others.

_____

_____

_____

91

You handle things when it hits the fan by acknowledging that things are happening. #OwnYourMistakes

_____

_____

_____

92

Accepting that you're in the middle
of a mess is the only way that you can
refocus your energy to fix the situation.
#OwnYourMistakes

_____

_____

_____

93

As soon as you accept that a situation is messy, you will be able to refocus your energy toward bringing all of your family, friends, and team together with you to solve the problem. #OwnYourMistakes

_____

_____

_____

94

The process of repairing starts when you embrace the mess. Make the mess your own, because something you did probably created it. Own it, love it, and fix it.

_____

_____

_____

95

To fix a messy situation, you must become vulnerable and transparent. The fix will come from both your efforts and the efforts of those around you whom you've helped.

_____

_____

_____

96

Accept the fact that you alone cannot fix a certain situation. Announce that you need help in a very loud and clear voice.

_____

_____

_____

97

The most powerful words in the English language are: please, thank you, and help. Don't be so arrogant that you think that you can fix it all by yourself.

_____

_____

_____

98

When you start sharing your predicament with others, the fix for the messy situation will become evident.

_____

_____

_____

99

When it hits the fan, you need to be strong enough to take responsibility, smart enough to know when you need help, and humble enough to ask for it.

_____

_____

_____

People don't care how much you know until they know how much you care. Do others know how much you care?

Bill Wallace
http://aha.pub/SuccessCatalyst

Share the AHA messages from this book socially by going to http://aha.pub/SuccessCatalyst.

Section VI

Spirituality, Family, and Friends

In life, we need to find the right balance between spirituality, family, and friends.

All three contribute greatly to who we are as individuals and how much we succeed. Without spirituality, family, and friends, our lives become empty shells, and that's a life devoid of happiness.

You control your own happiness, and you get to choose whom you're with. As we journey through life, we meet a lot of people with different personalities and different beliefs. If you want to live a well-rounded life, you need to accept other people for who they are, no matter how much they differ from you.

Watch this video: http://aha.pub/SuccessCatalystS6.

100

People don't care how much you know until they know how much you care. How do you show you care for others?

_____

_____

_____

101

Your family, friends, and spirituality should always be omnipresent. They're the lifeblood of a life worth living.

_____

_____

_____

102

Without spirituality, family, and friends,
there will be such a huge void, your
enjoyment of life will be short lived.

_____

_____

_____

103

When you have spirituality, family, and friends
as part of your daily walk and as part of your
vision, both for today and for the future, you
have a well-rounded, fulfilled,
rewarding, growth-focused life.

_____

_____

_____

104

It's hard to be successful in all of the other things you're doing in life if your spirituality, family, and friends are not in alignment. Are yours aligned?

_____

_____

_____

105

You have to surround yourself with like-minded people, as well as contrarians, to grow. You can't grow with your own fertilizer. You have to have other people fertilizing your field with different ideas and different mindsets.

_____

_____

_____

106

When you have family, friends, and spirituality aligned, you will be a better person. #BeBetter

_____

_____

_____

107

Being non-judgmental, focused, and helpful and having a good family, good friends, and a spiritual nature defines who you are as a person.

_____

_____

_____

108

Having a successful relationship involves finding out your similarities and respecting your differences. #RespectDifferences

_____

_____

_____

109

Be accepting of others although they may
be different from you. #RespectDifferences

_____

_____

_____

110

Differences in beliefs, skin color, and language don't matter. We are all human beings, and we're all bound to succeed if we can just get past those differences. #RespectDifferences

_____

_____

_____

111

Our strengths lie in differences, not in similarities. #RespectDifferences

_____

_____

_____

112

When you accept others as they are,
your life will be filled with peace.
#RespectDifferences

_____

_____

_____

113

It's not our differences that divide us, but
rather our inability to recognize, accept, and
celebrate them. #RespectDifferences

_____

_____

_____

114

Be a spiritual person, treasure your family,
and enjoy with your friends.
Live a good life. You deserve it!

_____

_____

_____

115

Fill your life with love. When you open your heart, you become a more understanding and accepting person.

_____

_____

_____

116

Success comes from the non-judgmental alignment of family, friends, and spirituality. Treat people well regardless of your differences.

_____

_____

_____

117

Success is finding a happy balance between family, friends, and spirituality. It's about the quality of life.

_____

_____

_____

118

Always pray to have eyes that see the best in people, a heart that forgives the worst, a mind that forgets the bad, and a soul that never loses spirit.

_____

_____

_____

Success is not the key to happiness. It's the other way around. Happiness is the key to success. If you love what you're doing, you will be successful.

Bill Wallace
http://aha.pub/SuccessCatalyst

Share the AHA messages from this book socially by going to
http://aha.pub/SuccessCatalyst.

Section VII

Words of Wisdom

If you hope to inspire others, whether you're in a leadership position or not, you need to understand that it all starts with you. It starts with you wanting to help other people and taking action. Inspire and be inspired by these nuggets of wisdom.

Always remember that a life lived for others is the only life worth living.

Watch this video: http://aha.pub/SuccessCatalystS7.

119

Be a success in your own eyes; it is not up to others to define what success is for you. Honor your commitments; your word, your heart, and your handshake define those commitments. Be a giver; it is all about others.

120

1 of 3 Principles to Live By: If it's not fun, don't do it. If you have to do it, find a way to make it fun first. You can!

121

2 of 3 Principles to Live By: Always a double win. If it ever ceases to be a double win, fix it or get out now, not tomorrow!

_____

_____

_____

122

3 of 3 Principles to Live By: I am always doing great. The definition of great may vary greatly from day to day, but I am always doing great!

_____

_____

_____

123

You can't define what success is for someone else. Doing that will just define what's not successful about you.

_____

_____

_____

124

Within each wall, there is an opportunity.
Look for it. It is called a door. Do you know
how to find and open the door to your
opportunity? #BreakThatWall

_____

_____

_____

125

The greatest success stories were created by people who recognized a problem and turned it into an opportunity.
@JoeSugarman
via http://aha.pub/BillWallace

_____

_____

_____

126

Each problem has hidden in it an opportunity so powerful that it literally dwarfs the problem. @JoeSugarman via http://aha.pub/BillWallace

_____

_____

_____

127

The squeaky wheel may get the grease, but it's also the first one to get replaced. Find a way to get yourself heard in a positive manner.

_____

_____

_____

128

The only difference between "Try" and
"Triumph" is a little "Umph."
Have a Triumphant Day!

_____

_____

_____

129

In a successful mentoring relationship,
you could end up learning more from your
mentee than your mentee has learned
from you.

_____

_____

_____

130

Work hard, play hard, have fun, and work some more.

_____

_____

_____

131

Let's have some fun, do some good, and make some money ... all at the same time.
@CharlesBahr via http://aha.pub/BillWallace

_____

_____

_____

132

Your actions speak so loudly, I cannot hear your words. @Ralph_W_Emerson via http://aha.pub/BillWallace

_____

_____

_____

133

What lies behind us and what lies before us are tiny matters compared to what lies within us.

_____

_____

_____

134

To finish first, more often than not, you will
have to put others ahead of yourself.

_____

_____

_____

135

A pure gift is one that is given from the heart to the right person at the right time at the right place with nothing expected in return.

_____

_____

_____

136

Do not try to fill the silence; it's already full. Just listen. It may be your spiritual self speaking to you.

_____

_____

_____

137

There is a life beyond success.
It's a life of giving back that success.

_____

_____

_____

138

Only a life lived for others is a life
worthwhile. @AlbertEinstein
via http://aha.pub/BillWallace

_____

_____

_____

139

There are three types of people: glass half full, glass half empty, and glass overflowing. Be someone who wants their glass to be so full that there's plenty to share with others.

_____

_____

_____

140

May you do what you love to do,
With people you love to do it with,
On purpose. God Bless and God Speed.

_____

_____

_____

Thank you for joining me on this journey
and sharing your time with me today.

Bill Wallace

About the Author

Bill Wallace
The founder and long-time leader of Success North Dallas, Bill Wallace has often said that his greatest skill is putting together the right people for the right reasons at the right time. Emanating from a rolodex that would put the US government to shame, Bill's generous "connection making" has benefited countless individuals who have turned to him for trusted referrals, strategic business support, educational mentorship, and business/leadership coaching as a Certified Professional Coach.

Bill's professional career flourished along with his development of the now thirty-year-old Success North Dallas, first as owner of Wallace Financial Group—a provider of business continuation planning, insurance, and financial strategies—and later, as Chairman and CEO of The Wallace Companies, a consulting firm specializing in capital development and executive management strategies. Bill currently serves on numerous boards and is Chairman of the Board of eQuine Holdings.

As a member of the Board of Governors of Northwood University and a strategic partner and board member of the University of North Texas Professional Leadership program, Bill continues to help aspiring college students forge successful careers in business and the community. In 2016, Northwood University honored him with an Honorary Doctorate of Laws (*honoris causa*) for his work in education, mentorship, and business excellence.

Bill is a charter member and past president of the Addison Rotary Club; an active member of the National Speaker's Association, C-Suite Network Advisors, and Hero Club; a past member of the Million Dollar Roundtable; and the author of the books, *Being a Catalyst for Success™: The Fulfilling Life of a Servant Leader* and *What about Who™* (June 2019). He has also served on the board of Ronald McDonald House Charities and the advisory boards of Alcuin Montessori School, Bryan's House, and Ronald McDonald House of Dallas. In recognition for his work in the community, The Art of Living Foundation and the International Association for Human Values honored Bill with the Heroes of Humanity Award in 2009.

AHAthat™

AHAthat makes it easy to share, author, and promote content. There are over 46,000 AHAmessages™ by thought leaders from around the world that you can share in seconds for free on Twitter, Facebook, LinkedIn, and Google+.

For those who want to author their own book, we have a 3-step, time-tested proven process that allows you to write your AHAbook™ of 140 digestible, bite-sized morsels and 5–8 blog posts. Once your content is on AHAthat, you have a customized link that you can use to have your fans/advocates share your content and help you grow your network.

⊃ Start sharing: **https://AHAthat.com**

⊃ Start authoring: **https://AHAthat.com/Author**

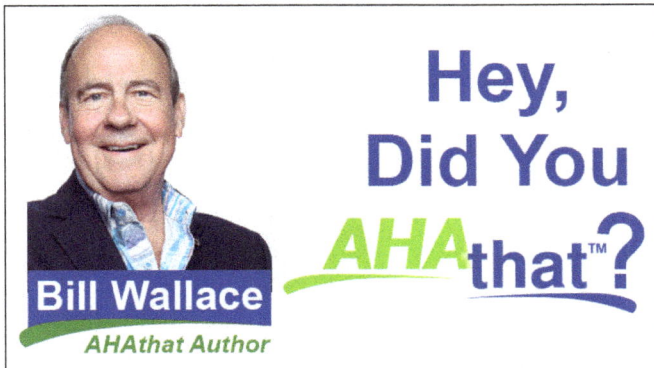

Please go directly to this book in AHAthat and share each AHAmessage socially at
http://aha.pub/SuccessCatalyst.

www.ingramcontent.com/pod-product-compliance
Lightning Source LLC
Chambersburg PA
CBHW071154200326
41519CB00018B/5227